This Book Belongs To:

**BY**
**Home Planners And Journals**

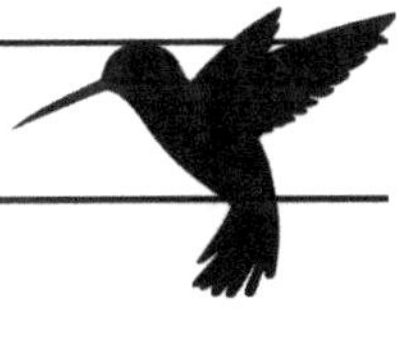

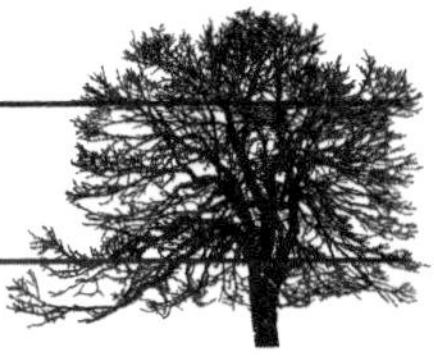

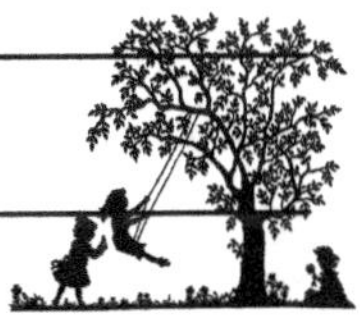

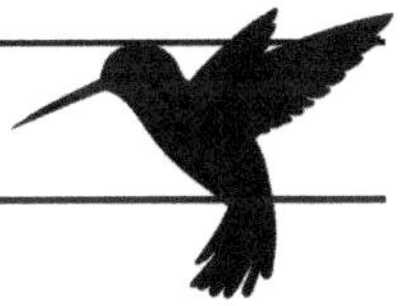

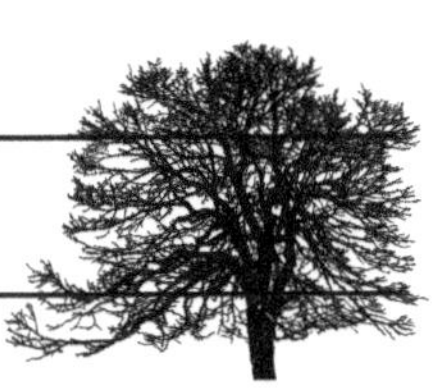

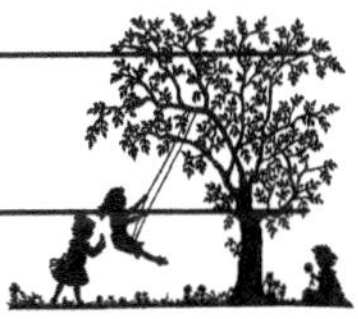

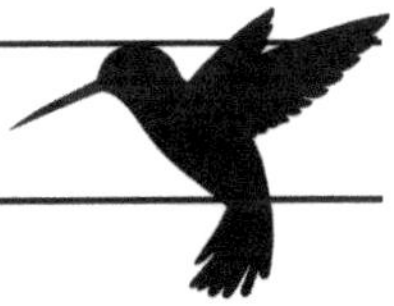

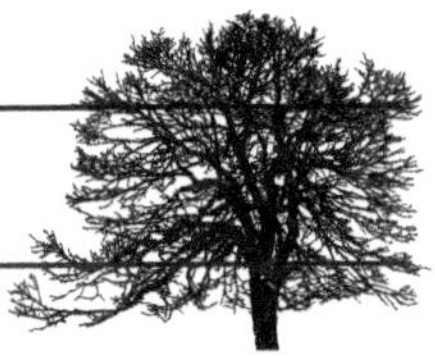

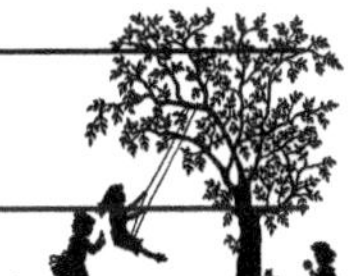

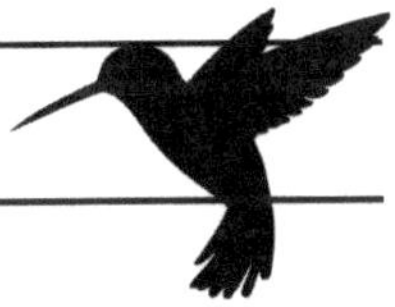

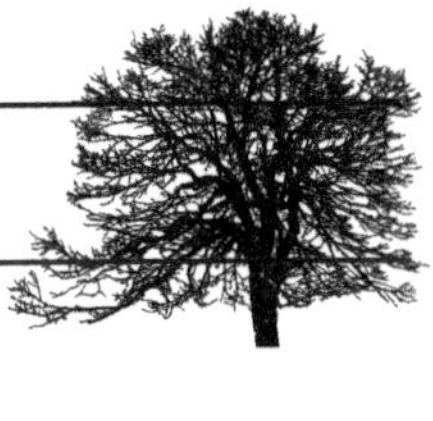

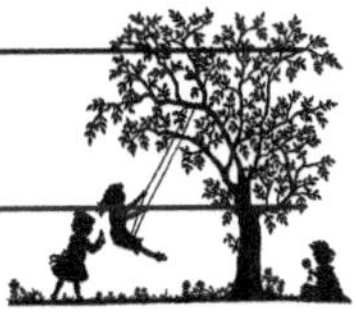

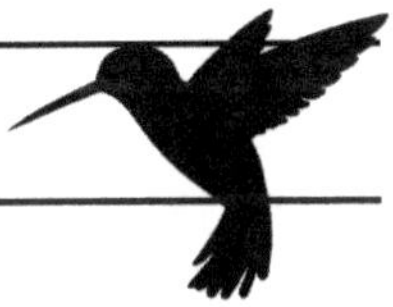

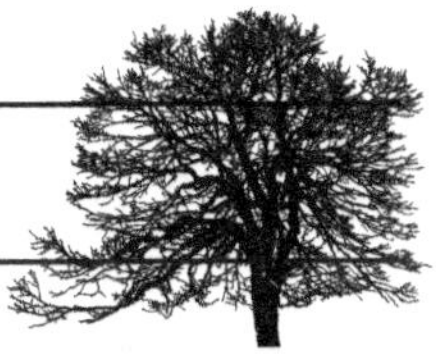

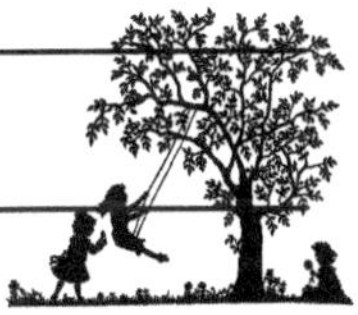

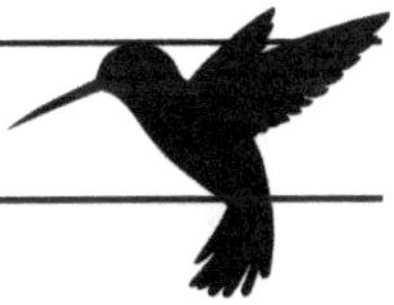

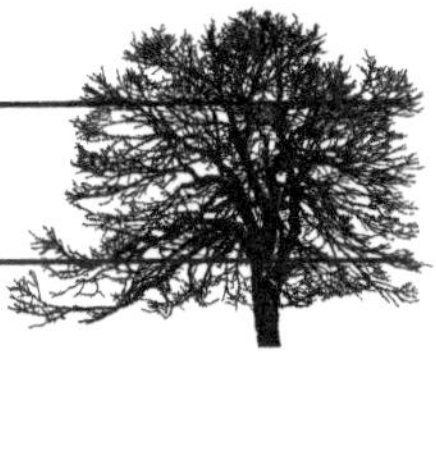

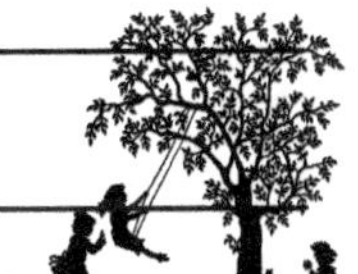

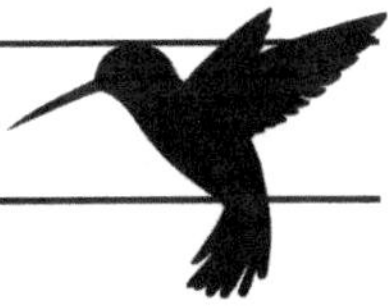

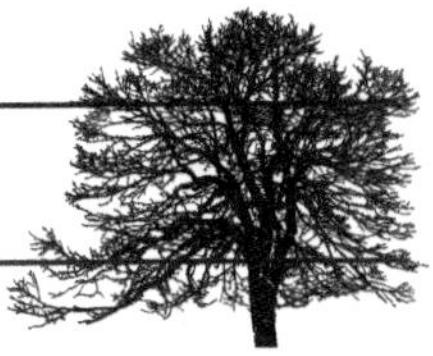

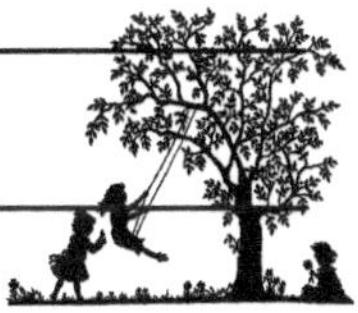

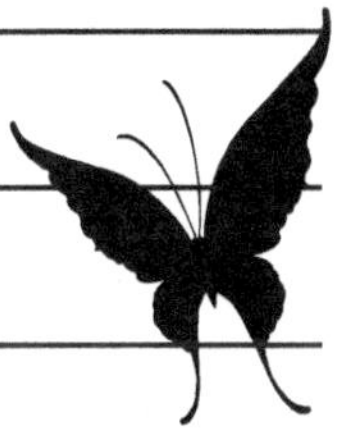

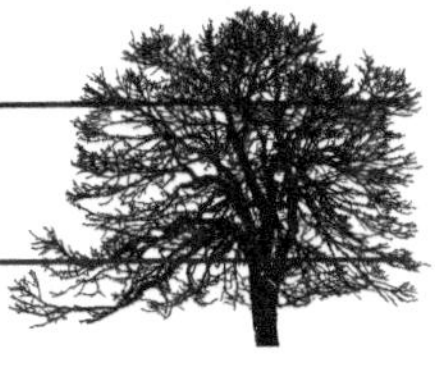

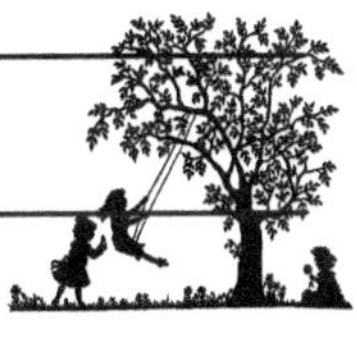

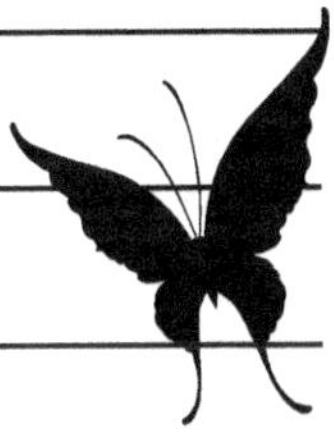

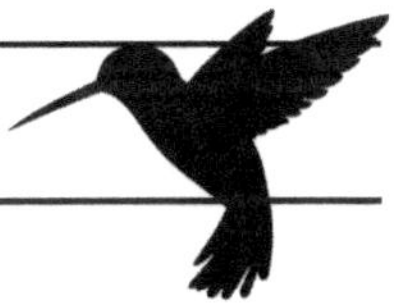

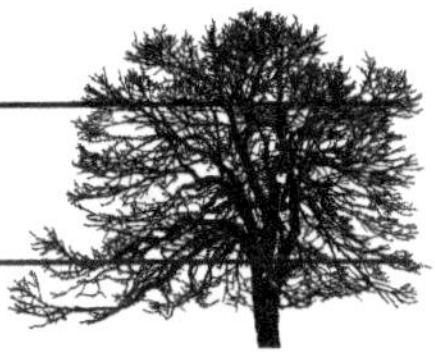

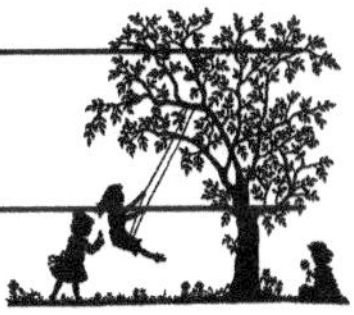

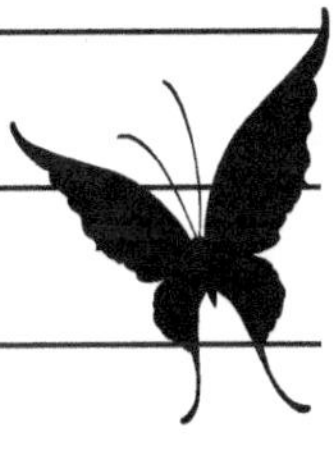

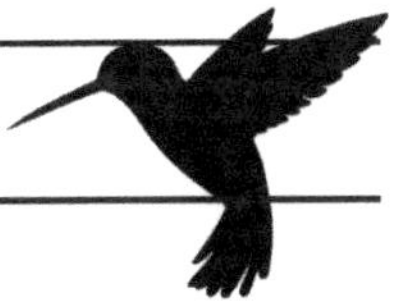

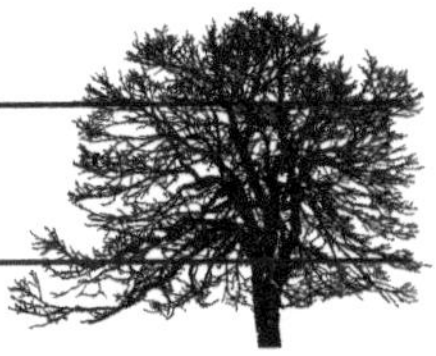

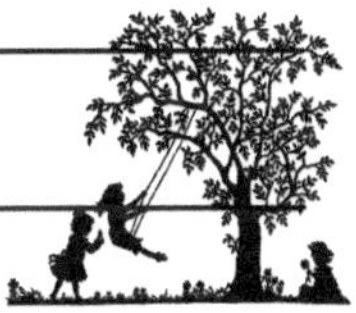

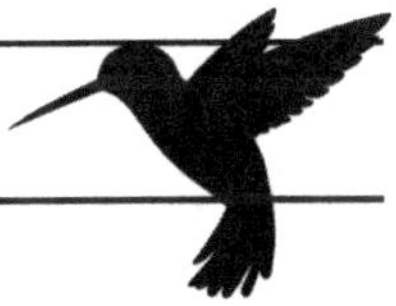

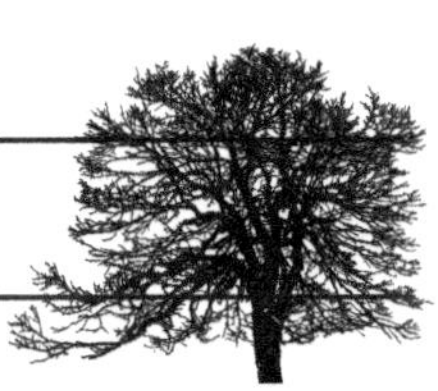

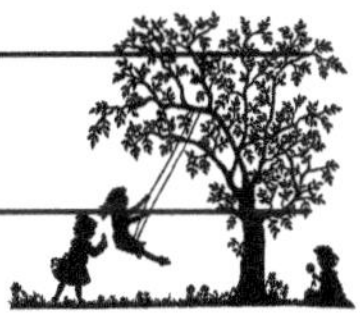

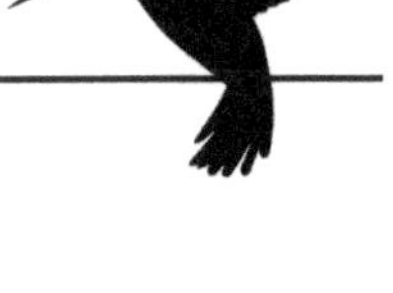

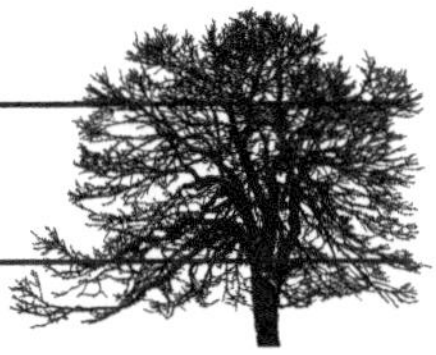

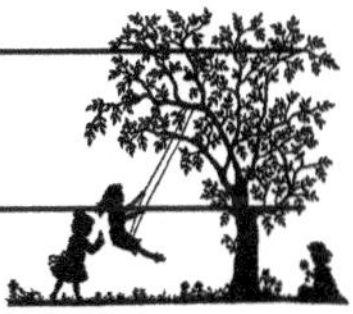

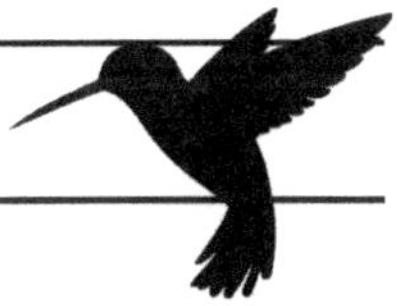

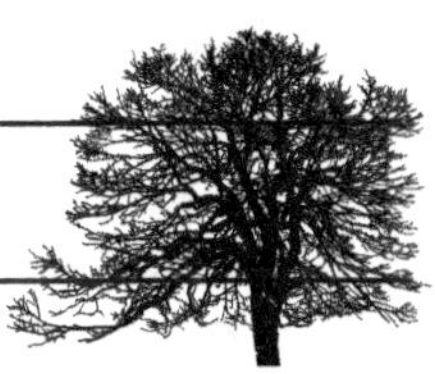

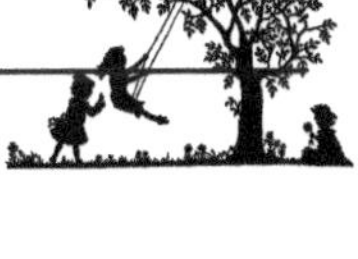

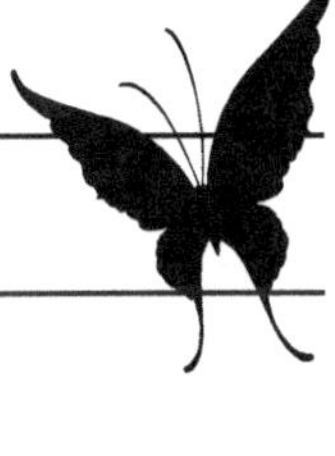

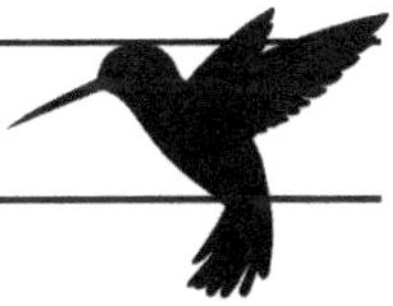

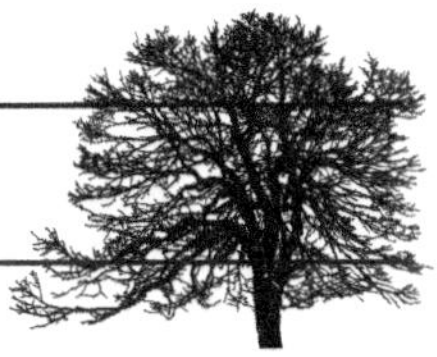

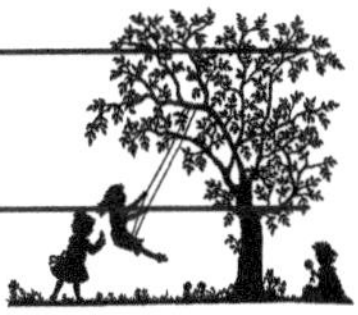

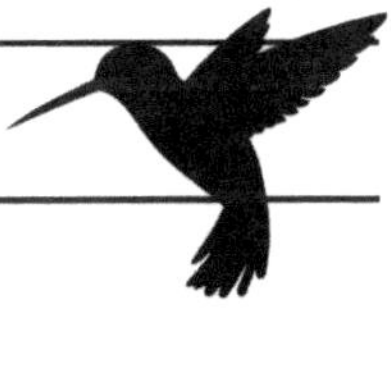

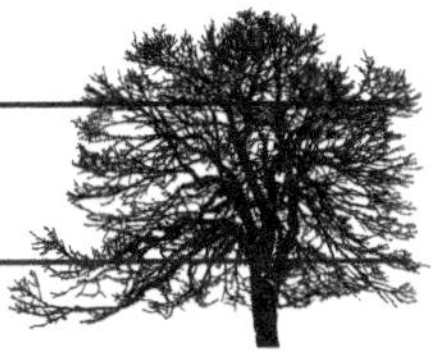

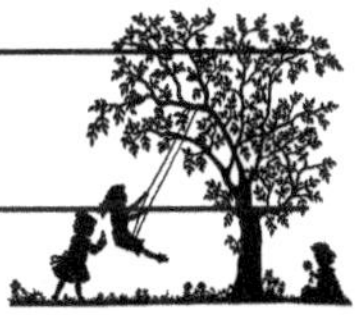

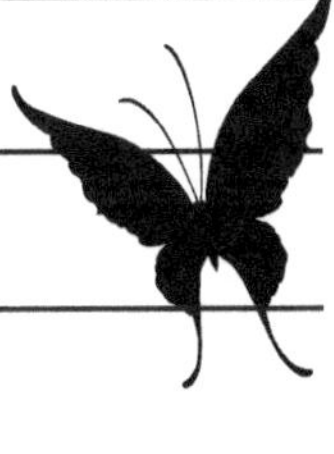

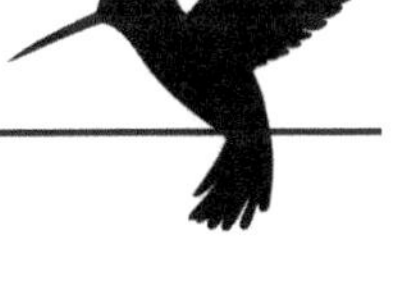

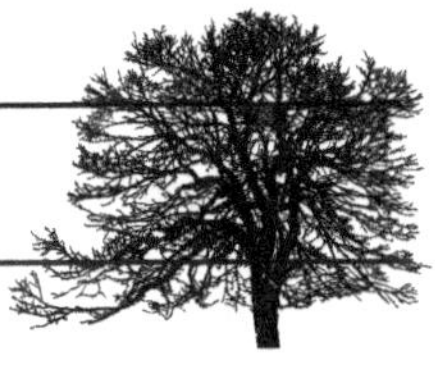

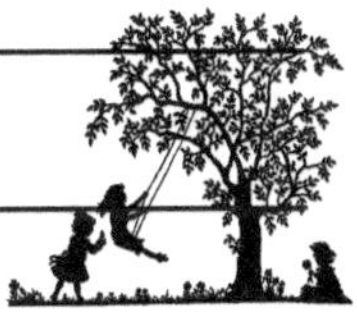

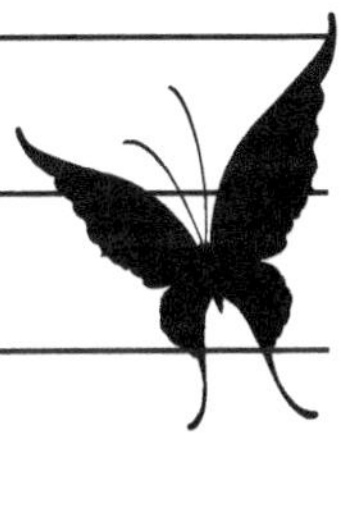

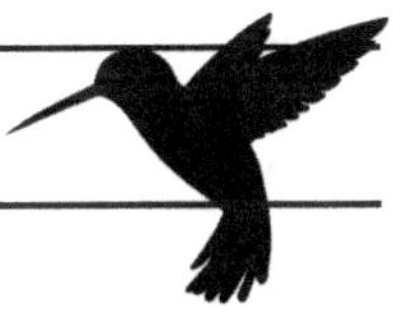

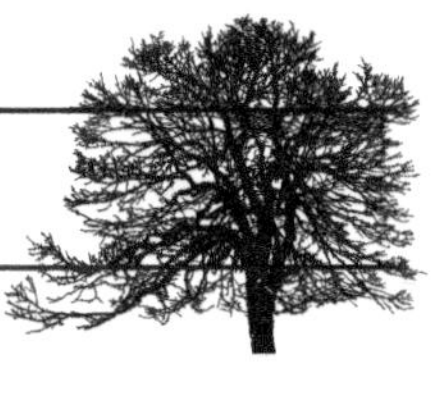

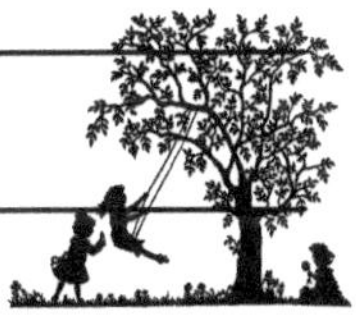

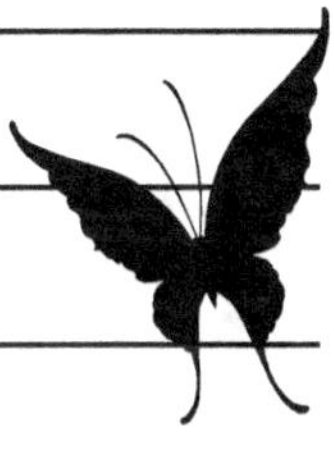

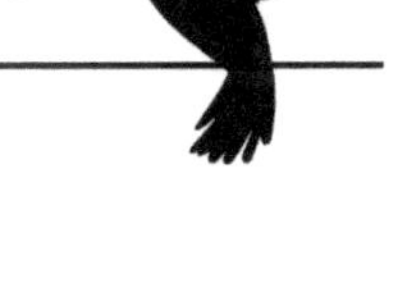

www.ingramcontent.com/pod-product-compliance
Lightning Source LLC
Chambersburg PA
CBHW072051280526
45788CB00006B/2260
*9781090232847*